EARTH'S ENERGY EXPERIMENTS

NATURAL GAS ENERGY PROJECTS

Easy Energy Activities for
Future Engineers!

JESSIE ALKIRE

CONSULTING EDITOR, DIANE CRAIG, M.A./READING SPECIALIST

Super Sandcastle

An Imprint of Abdo Publishing
abdopublishing.com

abdopublishing.com

Published by Abdo Publishing, a division of ABDO, PO Box 398166, Minneapolis, Minnesota 55439. Copyright © 2019 by Abdo Consulting Group, Inc. International copyrights reserved in all countries. No part of this book may be reproduced in any form without written permission from the publisher. Super SandCastle™ is a trademark and logo of Abdo Publishing.

Printed in the United States of America, North Mankato, Minnesota
052018
092018

Design and Production: Mighty Media, Inc.
Editor: Liz Salzmann
Cover Photographs: Mighty Media, Inc.; Shutterstock
Interior Photographs: iStockphoto; Mighty Media, Inc.; Shutterstock; Wikimedia Commons

The following manufacturers/names appearing in this book are trademarks: Anderson's, Artist's Loft™, Conair®, CVS Pharmacy®, Franklin®, Hostess® Twinkies®, Nice!™, PAM®, Play-Doh®, Pyrex®, Taylor®, Toysmith®

Library of Congress Control Number: 2017961708

Publisher's Cataloging-in-Publication Data

Names: Alkire, Jessie, author.
Title: Natural gas energy projects: Easy energy activities for future engineers! / by Jessie Alkire.
Other titles: Easy energy activities for future engineers!
Description: Minneapolis, Minnesota : Abdo Publishing, 2019. | Series: Earth's energy experiments
Identifiers: ISBN 9781532115639 (lib.bdg.) | ISBN 9781532156359 (ebook)
Subjects: LCSH: Natural gas as fuel--Juvenile literature. | Handicraft--Juvenile literature. | Science projects--Juvenile literature. | Earth sciences--Experiments--Juvenile literature.
Classification: DDC 553.285--dc23

Super SandCastle™ books are created by a team of professional educators, reading specialists, and content developers around five essential components—phonemic awareness, phonics, vocabulary, text comprehension, and fluency—to assist young readers as they develop reading skills and strategies and increase their general knowledge. All books are written, reviewed, and leveled for guided reading and early reading intervention programs for use in shared, guided, and independent reading and writing activities to support a balanced approach to literacy instruction.

TO ADULT HELPERS

The projects in this title are fun and simple. There are just a few things to remember to keep kids safe. Some projects require the use of hot objects. Also, kids may be using messy materials such as glue or paint. Make sure they protect their clothes and work surfaces. Review the projects before starting, and be ready to assist when necessary.

KEY SYMBOL

Watch for this warning symbol in this book. Here is what it means.

HOT!
You will be working with something hot. Get help!

CONTENTS

WHAT IS NATURAL GAS?

Natural gas is a **fossil fuel**. It comes from ancient plant and animal remains. The remains were buried underground. Heat and pressure changed the remains. This **released** natural gas.

Natural gas gets trapped in underground rock. In some places, natural gas escapes above ground. It burns easily.

BURNING NATURAL GAS

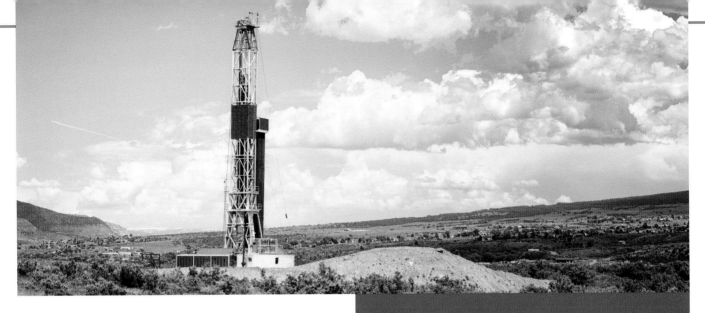

NATURAL GAS DRILLING RIG

People drill into the ground to remove natural gas. Gas is moved through long pipelines to processing plants. Then the gas can be used for electricity and heating.

Gas is a popular energy today. But it isn't a renewable **resource**. There is a limited supply of natural gas.

Also, burning natural gas **releases greenhouse gases**. These gases harm the **environment**. Scientists are working on reducing this effect.

NATURAL GAS PIPELINE

DRILLING FOR NATURAL GAS

Before natural gas can be used, it must be found and collected. Scientists use several methods to detect natural gas underground. Then they use different drilling methods to remove it.

FINDING NATURAL GAS

Natural gas is usually deep underground. It can be hard to discover. So, scientists study the rocks in an area. They might set off explosions. Then, they study the sound waves and **vibrations** from the explosions. This can help them tell whether there is natural gas in the area.

CONVENTIONAL DRILLING

One way to drill for natural gas is **conventional** drilling. It is used for gas that is in shallower rock layers, such as sandstone. The drill goes straight into the rock. The natural pressure underground pushes the gas up through a well.

FRACKING

Some natural gas is in hard **shale** rock deep underground. This gas is mined using a process called fracking. Liquid and sand is shot into the shale. This creates cracks in the shale so the gas can escape. Then the gas moves up through a well.

NATURAL GAS HISTORY

Natural gas has been used for centuries. In the 500s, people in China used natural gas to boil seawater. Natural gas started being used for lighting in the 1700s and 1800s.

Natural gas was used only for lighting for many years. Then, Robert Bunsen invented the Bunsen burner. This burner showed that gas could be used for heating and cooking.

GAS LAMPS

ROBERT BUNSEN

Robert Bunsen was a German scientist. He was also a science teacher. He spent much of his time in his lab. Bunsen made many important discoveries. But he is most famous for inventing the Bunsen burner in 1855. The burner combined gas and air to create a flame. The Bunsen burner is still used in schools and laboratories today!

BUNSEN BURNER

Natural gas quickly became a common energy in homes and businesses. It is mostly used for heating and in **appliances** such as gas stoves. But it can also be used to create electricity.

Natural gas is cleaner than other **fossil fuels**. Experts believe natural gas might become the world's main source of energy.

MATERIALS

Here are some of the materials that you will need for the projects in this book.

BAKING PAN

COOKING SPRAY

DRINKING STRAWS

DUCT TAPE

FUNNEL

GELATIN POWDER

HAIR DRYER

KITCHEN SCALE

LETTUCE

LOAF PAN

MAPLE SYRUP

MASKING TAPE

MEASURING CUPS

MEASURING SPOONS

OVEN MITTS

PAPER CUPS

PING-PONG BALLS

PLASTIC BOTTLE

PLAY-DOH

PUSHPINS

ROCK KIT

STAPLER

SYRINGE

TUNA

TWINKIES

GAS MOLECULE MOVEMENT

MATERIALS: newspaper, paint, paintbrush, 12 white ping-pong balls, wire basket with openings smaller than the ping-pong balls, cardboard, scissors, masking tape, 6 boxes, hair dryer

Gas **molecules** are always in motion. This motion is affected by heat and pressure. The motion causes gas to rise through layers of underground rock.

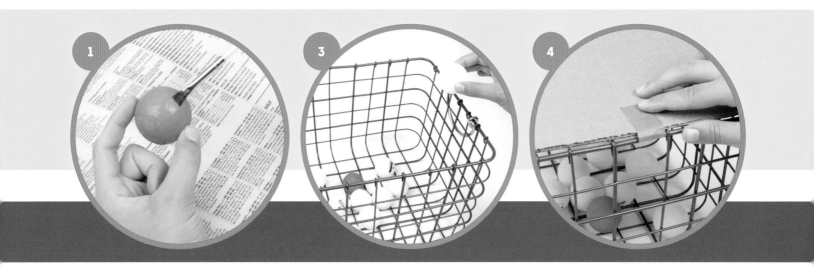

① Cover your work surface with newspaper. Paint one ping-pong ball a bright color. Let it dry.

② Cut a piece of cardboard the same size as the top of the wire basket.

③ Put the ping-pong balls in the basket. The balls represent gas **molecules**.

④ Tape the cardboard over the top of the basket.

⑤ Make two equal towers of boxes. Set the basket across the towers.

⑥ Point the hair dryer up at the bottom of the basket. Turn it on. The hair dryer represents underground heat and pressure.

⑦ Watch the gas molecules move! Keep an eye on the colored ball to see how one gas molecule behaves.

⑧ Try changing the speed of the hair dryer. Or move the hair dryer closer to or farther away from the basket. This changes the amount of heat and pressure. What happens to the molecules?

GAS BALLOON BLOW-UP

MATERIALS: 3 paper cups, kitchen scale, canned tuna, spoon, empty plastic bottle, lettuce, sand, funnel, pond or creek water, measuring spoons, balloon, duct tape

Not all natural gas is produced below ground. Natural gas also forms when plant and animal remains **decompose**. Tiny organisms break down these materials. This produces natural gas.

① Put a cup on the scale. Set the scale to zero grams.

② Put 10 grams of tuna in the cup.

③ Put the tuna in the plastic bottle.

④ Tear up a few lettuce leaves. Put the pieces in the bottle.

Continued on the next page.

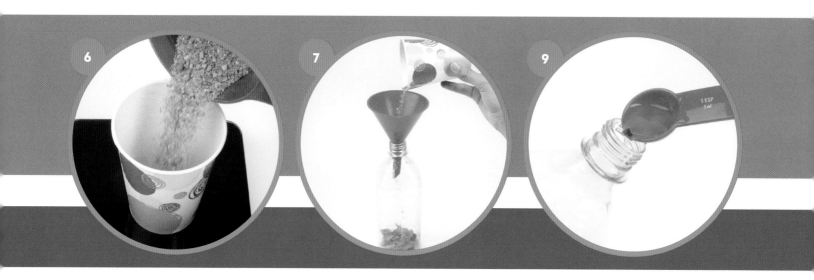

5 Put another cup on the scale. Set the scale to zero grams.

6 Measure 50 grams of sand.

7 Use a funnel to pour the sand into the bottle.

8 Have an adult help you get a small cup of water from a pond or creek.

9 Put 2 teaspoons of pond or creek water in the bottle. Tip the bottle so the water flows down the side instead of straight down.

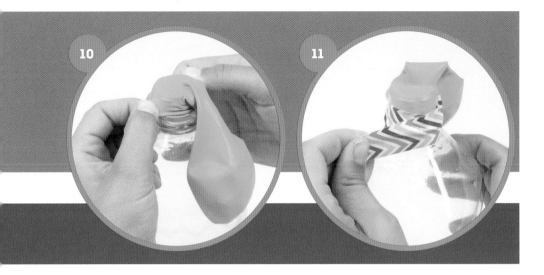

10 Stretch the neck of the balloon over the top of the bottle.

11 Use duct tape to secure the balloon to the bottle.

12 Place the bottle in a warm place out of the way. Check on it each day and observe any changes. After a few days, the balloon should start to fill with air!

DIGGING DEEPER

In this experiment, the lettuce represents dead plants. The tuna represents dead animals. The sand and water represent the ocean that buries the remains.

Over time, the remains start to rot. This is a chemical process that creates natural gas. The gas takes up more room than the air in the bottle. This causes some of the air to be pushed into the balloon.

POROUS ROCKS

MATERIALS: rock kit (with sandstone, shale, limestone, granite, slate & marble), baking pan, oven, oven mitts, kitchen scale, notebook, pencil, 6 paper cups, water

Some rocks are more likely to **contain** natural gas than others. **Porous** rocks are most likely to contain gas. This is because they have more spaces for gas and other materials to enter.

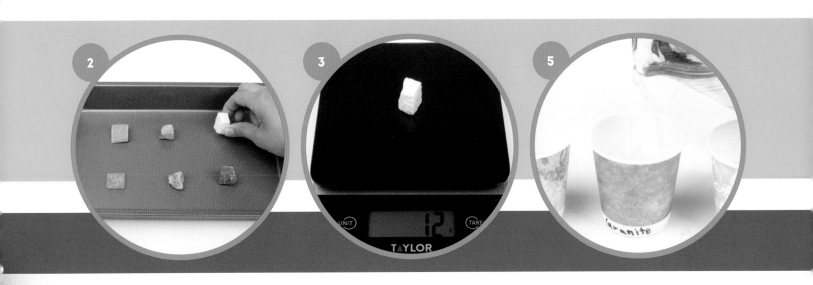

① Preheat the oven to 200 **degrees** Fahrenheit.

② Place the rocks in the pan. Bake them for 2 hours. This removes any moisture. Let the rocks cool.

③ Weigh each rock on a kitchen scale. Record the measurements in a notebook.

④ Write the name of each type of rock on a paper cup. Place each rock in its cup.

⑤ Put water in each cup to cover the rocks.

⑥ Let the rocks sit in the water for at least 1 hour.

⑦ Remove the rocks from the water. Weigh each rock again. Record the measurements in the notebook.

⑧ Think about the results. Did the weight of any of the rocks change? Which changed the most? Which changed the least?

PLAY-DOH CORE SAMPLING

MATERIALS: 4 colors of Play-Doh, paper cup, plastic drinking straws

Scientists have ways to look for natural gas. One way is core sampling. In this process, a drill removes a sample of underground rock layers. Then, scientists can check the removed rock and soil for natural gas.

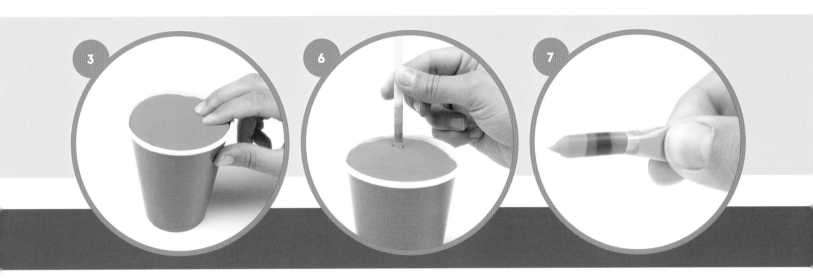

① Break the Play-Doh into 16 pieces. Make the pieces different sizes.

② Put all but one piece of Play-Doh in the cup. Mix up the colors. Press firmly to pack the pieces down tightly.

③ Flatten the last piece of Play-Doh. Press it over the other pieces. This is Earth's surface.

④ Decide which color will represent rock that **contains** natural gas.

⑤ Slowly push the straw into the Play-Doh. Turn the straw as you push it down.

⑥ Slowly take the straw out of the Play-Doh. Turn the straw as you pull it up.

⑦ Squeeze the straw where the Play-Doh ends. Slide your fingers toward the end of the straw to push the Play-Doh out. This is your core sample.

⑧ Look at the layers in your sample. Is the rock containing natural gas included?

⑨ Keep taking samples from different spots until you find natural gas.

SNACK CAKE DRILLING

MATERIALS: 2 Twinkies, plate, 2 bendable drinking straws, scissors, ruler, pencil, notebook

Once natural gas is found underground, it usually needs to be removed by drilling. There are two common ways to drill for natural gas. These are vertical and **horizontal** drilling.

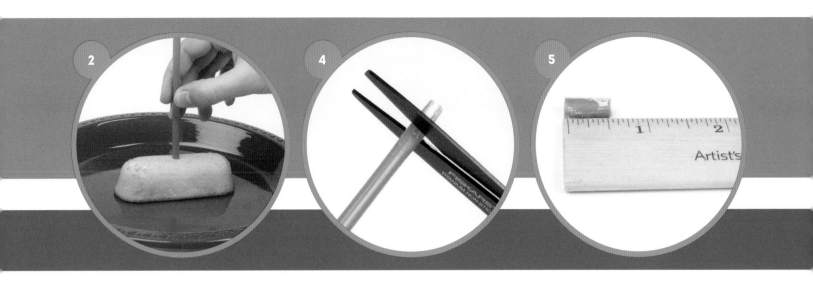

① Set an unwrapped Twinkie on a plate.

② Push a straw into the top of the Twinkie. Turn the straw as you push it down. This is vertical drilling.

③ Remove the straw.

④ Cut the straw where the filling ends.

⑤ Measure the cut-off piece of straw. Record the measurement in a notebook.

⑥ Place the second Twinkie on a plate. Push the short end of a straw into the top of the Twinkie. Remove the straw.

Continued on the next page.

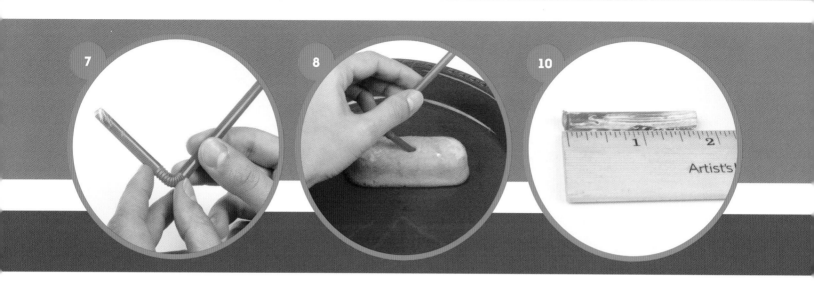

7 Bend the straw into an angle like the corner of a square.

8 Push the short end of the straw back into the hole. Instead of pushing straight down, push the straw toward one end of the Twinkie. This is **horizontal** drilling.

9 Remove the straw. Cut the straw where the filling ends.

10 Measure the cut-off piece of straw. Record the measurement in a notebook.

11 Compare the vertical and horizontal drilling measurements. Which method collected more filling?

12 Enjoy the drilled Twinkies as a snack!

DIGGING DEEPER

Vertical and **horizontal** drilling are the most common ways to drill for natural gas. Vertical drilling is drilling straight down into the ground. Horizontal drilling begins like vertical drilling. But then the drill turns sideways to drill horizontally. Horizontal drilling can often reach more natural gas than vertical drilling.

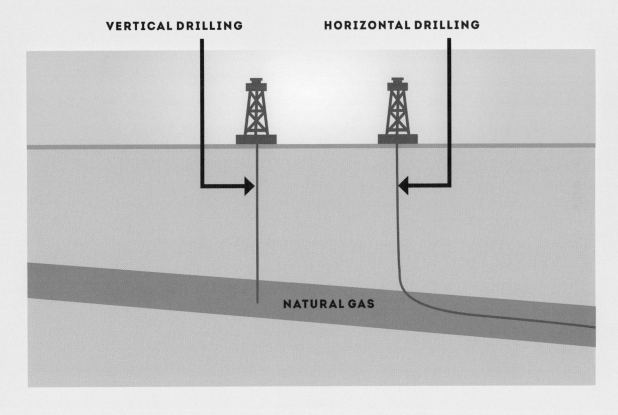

VERTICAL DRILLING   HORIZONTAL DRILLING

NATURAL GAS

GELATIN FRACKING

MATERIALS: measuring cups, water, medium bowl, unflavored gelatin powder, spoon, cooking spray, loaf pan, refrigerator, plate, 2 plastic drinking straws, stapler, duct tape, pushpin, syringe, maple syrup

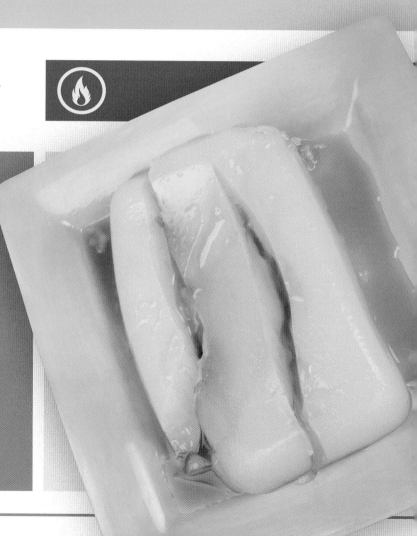

You learned about fracking on page 7. Now see how it works by fracking with gelatin and syrup! In this experiment, the gelatin represents **shale** rock. The syrup represents fracking liquid.

① Pour ½ cup of tap water into the bowl.

② Add 0.75 ounces (21 g) of unflavored gelatin powder.

③ Boil 3½ cups of water. Carefully pour it into the bowl. Stir until the gelatin **dissolves**.

④ Coat the inside of the loaf pan with cooking spray. Pour the gelatin mixture into the loaf pan.

⑤ Put the pan in the refrigerator for about 4 hours or until the gelatin sets.

Continued on the next page.

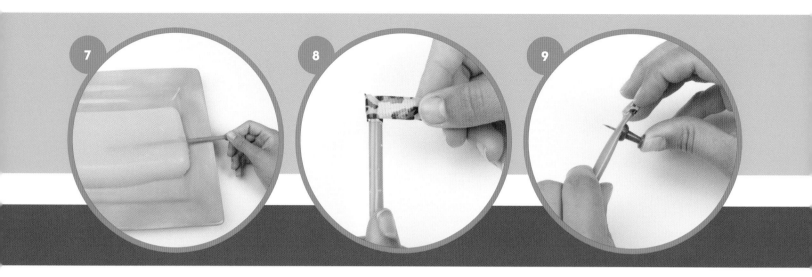

6 Take the gelatin out of the refrigerator. Set a plate upside down on the loaf pan. Turn the plate and pan over together so the plate is on the bottom. Lift the loaf pan off of the gelatin.

7 Push one of the straws into the side of the gelatin. Push it about two-thirds of the way through the block. Remove the straw and set it aside.

8 Staple one end of the second straw closed. Wrap duct tape around the stapled end.

9 Poke a pushpin through the straw five times. Start near the taped end. Space the holes about ½ inch (1.3 cm) apart.

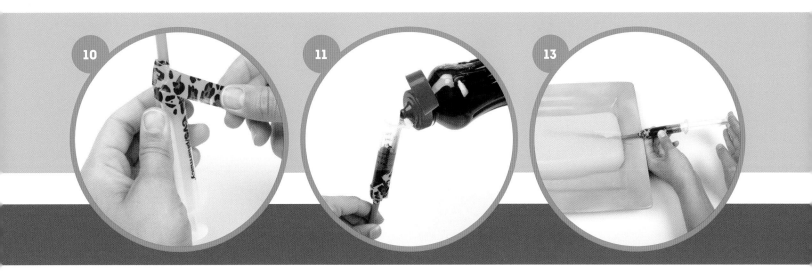

10 Stick the end of the syringe into the open end of the straw. Tape it in place.

11 Remove the plunger from the syringe. Pour maple syrup into the syringe. Make sure the syrup fills both the straw and the syringe.

12 Place the plunger back in the syringe.

13 Push the end of the straw into the hole you made in step 7.

14 Quickly push the plunger. This shoots the syrup into the gelatin.

15 Observe how the gelatin changes. Shoot syrup into the gelatin in a few other spots. What happens?

CONCLUSION

Natural gas is an important energy source. It is used for heating and electricity. It is one of the most popular **fossil fuels**. But natural gas has harmful effects on the **environment**. Scientists are exploring ways to solve this problem.

QUIZ

2 Burning natural gas produces **greenhouse gases**.
TRUE OR FALSE?

3 From what kind of rock does fracking remove natural gas?

3 Where are Bunsen burners used today?

LEARN MORE ABOUT IT!

You can find out more about natural gas energy at the library. Or you can ask an adult to help you **research** natural gas energy on the internet!

Answers: 1. True   2. Shale   3. Schools and laboratories

GLOSSARY

appliance – a machine that does a particular job.

contain – to consist of or include.

conventional – following the usual or widely accepted way of doing something.

decompose – to break down or rot.

degree – the unit used to measure temperature.

dissolve – to become part of a liquid.

environment – nature and everything in it, such as the land, sea, and air.

fossil fuel – a fuel formed in Earth from the remains of plants or animals. Coal, oil, and natural gas are fossil fuels.

greenhouse gas – a gas, such as carbon dioxide, that traps heat in Earth's atmosphere.

horizontal – in the same direction as the ground, or side to side.

molecule – a group of two or more atoms that make up the smallest piece of a substance.

porous – having small holes that allow air or liquid to pass through.

release – to set free or let out.

research – to find out more about something.

resource – something that is usable or valuable.

shale – a kind of rock formed from clay and mud that splits easily into flat pieces.

vibration – a series of small, fast movements back and forth.